Developing Your
Asking
Rights

The Most Important Questions Your Organization Needs to Answer
to Ensure You Have Earned the Right to Successfully Ask for Money

Tom Ralser

Developing Your *Asking Rights*: The Most Important Questions Your Organization Needs to Answer to Ensure You Have Earned the Right to Successfully Ask for Money

Published by That Dog Won't Hunt Press

Printed in the United States.

First Printing 2016.

ISBN: 978-0-9898358-1-7

That Dog Won't Hunt Press
520 Sheritan Way
Smyrna, GA 30082

www.AskingRights.com

Developing Your
Asking Rights

The Most Important Questions
Your Organization Needs to Answer
to Ensure You Have Earned the Right
to Successfully Ask for Money

Preface

Since publishing "*Asking Rights*: Why Some Nonprofits Get Funded (and some don't)" in 2013, the workshops, speaking engagements, and pre-campaign client work in which I have participated encouraged me to develop various written exercises that more effectively illustrate specific concepts offered in the book. At times, I use several exercises together to illuminate ideas, while in other instances one exercise is all that is needed.

The thought behind making the worksheets available together in this format is so that workshop and conference participants—as well as nonprofit board members and staff—can take advantage or revisit them after my time with them comes to a close. This workbook, as a companion to the book, contains the most road-tested of my exercises. They are presented in an order that takes a department or organization step-by-step through the process of discovering what might be hindering funding success and how to make full use of the potential that *Asking Rights* allows.

HAPPY ASKING!!!

TOM RALSER
AUTHOR

TABLE OF CONTENTS

The *ASKING RIGHTS* Concept

All nonprofits have the legal right to ask you for money.
Not all of them have *Asking Rights*.

This was the first 'key concept' outlined in the book "*Asking Rights*: Why Some Nonprofits Get Funded (and some don't)." It sprang from an ill-fated yet stubbornly pervasive notion that I saw repeated throughout the nonprofit industry: "People will give money to my organization because it's doing good things."

Having raised money for all shapes and sizes of nonprofits over the past 20 years, I tell you—emphatically—that the above notion is <u>*not*</u> only untrue, it is a harmful construct that stands in the way of an organization reaching its mission-critical potential. When a nonprofit board and staff truly understand how to *earn* the right to ask for money—when people take the time to embrace the specific steps that lead to sustainable funding success—the organization's ability to do "good things" exponentially expands.

In the book, I presented three introductions to illustrate the need for greater awareness about the deliberate actions that help and/or hurt all funding efforts. The two more concise versions are below.

The 100 Word Introduction
Nobody likes to see their hard-earned money wasted. Yet when it comes to giving money to nonprofits, many people seem to turn a blind eye to the reality that not every nonprofit is a good steward with the money they are given. Not that they steal it, or that anything unseemly or illegal is going on, but that they are simply not impacting the world as the giver was led to believe. This lack of impact (or effectiveness), becomes most obvious when one is asking funders for money. That's when the real discussion takes place.

The One Sentence Introduction
It's all about the outcomes.

As the following exercises will prove, the importance of outcomes cannot—and should not—be underestimated. They are *why* people ultimately give money to nonprofits, and sustainable funding depends on valuable outcomes being delivered. *Asking Rights* allows these truisms to be translated into actions and the positive effects realized for the full benefit of an effective nonprofit organization.

Q: WHAT ARE *ASKING RIGHTS?*

A: *Asking Rights* are the ability of a nonprofit to deliver outcomes that are valuable to investors.

There are many significant words in the above answer.

➤ *Deliver:* The nonprofit must actually deliver on its promise of results, not just print glossy marketing materials repeating its mission and goals.

➤ *Outcomes:* Organizational results need to simply demonstrate how they impact their primary customers' lives, not just offer measures of activity that describe how money was spent.

➤ *Valuable:* The outcomes need to be valuable in that they are meaningful to those who invest to make them possible.

➤ *Investors:* These are the individuals, companies, organizations, and foundations that make the intended outcomes possible through financial investment.

Investment, as opposed to gift or donation, is used to indicate an expectation of performance. The ability to deliver valuable outcomes—to perform as a mission-based organization—is more difficult than it may sound. Every nonprofit, when asked if it delivers outcomes, answers in the affirmative. But often the outcomes a nonprofit chooses to highlight are not the ones seen as valuable by those being asked to write a check. Of greater issue is when a nonprofit has a hard time helping investors quickly and easily connect the dots from dollars to outcomes. When it comes to value, complexity is not an asset. It's actually an inverse relationship: as complexity goes up, funding goes down.

An even more important question is...

Q: WHY BOTHER WITH *ASKING RIGHTS*?

A: Long-term, sustainable funding for a nonprofit is best achieved by consistently delivering valuable outcomes.

In communities where I have delivered workshops and seminars about sustainable funding plans, return on investment (ROI)-based funding models, and investable outcomes, some nonprofits have taken on my vernacular, e.g. referring to donors as 'investors.' But simply adopting a new vocabulary does not earn *Asking Rights*. Saying you will deliver outcomes—the impact your organization has on the lives of its primary customers—because you perceive they are valued by investors is vastly different and far less difficult than actually delivering them.

To develop a truly long-term, sustainable funding model—one that can generate investment for years to come—an organization must deliver valuable outcomes or investors will fund an organization that does.

The Development Director found herself searching for the right answer.
She never realized it would be so difficult to raise money.

How would you answer this question?

Certain pages in this book are left blank. Feel free to use them for notes!

HOW TO USE THIS WORKBOOK

This workbook is divided into two major sections.

PART 1 THE INGREDIENTS

This section contains 15 worksheets to help you understand the three main components of *Asking Rights.*

➢ Credibility
➢ Fundraising Skills
➢ Outcomes

PART 2 THE RECIPE

This section contains 10 worksheets that lay out the action steps needed to integrate the above 'ingredients' into a successful campaign using my exclusive Investment-Driven Model for fundraising.

➢ Discovering Investor Motivations
➢ Translating Your Outcomes To Value
➢ Matching Your Value To Investor Motivations
➢ Using Campaign Dynamics To Maximize Funding

IMPORTANT POINTS

▪ The steps presented on the following pages are predicated on the assumption that funding is needed by your organization and some version of a funding campaign is in the organization's future. By this I mean that, at some point, a program of work will be presented to potential funders, a campaign leadership team will be assembled, and in-person 'asks' will be made to raise capital.

▪ This workbook often refers to a 'campaign.' Keep in mind I use this word interchangeably with the phrase 'strategic initiative,' which I actually favor. *Campaign* sounds laborious. *Strategic initiative* sounds as if a group of people came together and proactively outlined a new and innovative program of work that is not the status quo.

▪ In this workbook, a capital campaign does not necessarily mean a campaign to build something, i.e. a 'bricks and mortar' campaign. A capital campaign, for our purposes, is an effort that fits the following criteria: large amounts of money pledged over multi-year periods.

▪ This workbook is most useful for those who are actively involved in the 'ask,' regardless of title or role...from CEO to development staff to board member.

- As with the book "*Asking Rights*: Why Some Nonprofits Get Funded (and some don't)," this companion workbook focuses on the process of raising money effectively. It is not intended to describe how to better manage your nonprofit, nor—and perhaps more important—is it preaching about the *theory* of fundraising. All the exercises in this book have been tested in the campaign trenches of raising money in today's competitive economy.

- While not intended to replace strategic planning for an organization, the exercises in this workbook prove that a sustainable funding approach CANNOT be achieved without it being a foundational element of the organization's overall strategy. Equally significant is the need to involve current and potential future investors in the strategic planning process so they understand the need for increased and sustained funding. As Ben Franklin aptly said, "By failing to prepare, you are preparing to fail."

- Last, the idea and format of this workbook pays homage to Peter Drucker's *The Five Most Important Questions You Will Ever Ask About Your Nonprofit Organization*, which is known now as *The Drucker Foundation Self-Assessment Tool*. His book is a timeless classic for any organization. It's simple, yet at the same time profound and effective. If you have not read it, I highly recommend you do.

PART 1
THE INGREDIENTS

Credibility
+ Fundraising Skills
+ Outcomes
_____
Asking Rights

C = CREDIBILITY

Definition	The quality or power of inspiring belief [i]
Critical Fundraising Advantage	It gets you in the door
Time Reference	Past and/or present
Encompasses	Visibility in the community, previous fundraising efforts, board strength, executive leadership, strength of brand, delivering on past promises, track record

It has often been said that the *Credibility* of an organization is what gets a fundraiser in the door. This point is difficult to argue and, as a generalized statement, is true. A foot in the door when combined with the other two variables in the *Asking Rights* equation—*Fundraising Skills* and *Outcomes*—more often than not allows for substantial dollars to be raised. To further the point, *Credibility* is an almost unshakeable belief that the organization does 'good things.'

For an example based on personal experience, I am happy to share with you that I am drawn to Goodwill Industries because of its *Credibility*. As an organization, it has convinced me over the years that it does 'good things' with my donations of clothing, sporting equipment, household items, etc. It makes dropping off my donations almost effortless, even to the point of providing a covered drive-through at some locations. After I unload my items, I am handed a receipt that allows me to go online and keep a permanent history of my donations. I can, literally, pull up, drop off, and be gone in a minute or less.

On Goodwill's website, there is a Donation Impact Calculator that gives me instant feedback on my actions. That feedback contains the name of a real person, a picture of that person (so they are hitting on the emotional cylinders), and a statistic that tells me what my donation will do, such as 50 minutes of financial planning classes for Ms. Johnson or 2.5 hours of a resume writing class for Mr. Smith. This nice touch may make me feel better about my decision to donate to Goodwill versus some other organization, but it is not what keeps me coming back. I donate to Goodwill because of previous *Credibility* that was established long ago and is reinforced during and after every visit.

A nonprofit branding consultant once told me that a nonprofit's brand is embodied in the feeling that I get when I hear the organization's name. In the case of Goodwill, that is certainly true for me. I believe they are doing good things and I believe I am helping them do good things. But what keeps me donating is the fact that the organization offers me transparent proof via online impact stories of how my donations provide critical support to its primary customers.

The next five worksheets focus on *Credibility*...on what it means in a fundraising context and how it can be improved to develop *Asking Rights*.

CREDIBILITY

Worksheet 1 What Makes You Credible?

A common definition of *Credibility* is "the quality of being believable or worthy of trust." In this instance, *Credibility* refers to your organization being worthy of a person's or organization's money. Understanding your organization's current level of *Credibility* begins with knowing how it is perceived by others.

Below are some questions to help you articulate the image you believe you are portraying in your area(s) of service and in your funding community.

- What makes your organization valuable to the community?
- What changes have happened in the community because of your organization's efforts?
- What changes have been made in the lives of people, animals, community groups, etc. because of your organization?
- What value has your organization added to an existing program or how has it helped provide a solution?
- What comes to mind when people think of your organization?
- What recognition or awards has the organization received?

A. List the top five factors that you feel gives your organization the *Credibility* to ask for large investments.

1. _____

2. _____

3. _____

4. _____

5. _____

B. Now describe *why* you feel each of the above factors makes your organization credible or gives your organization *Credibility*? (Note: There may be several 'whys' for one factor.)

Factor   Why?

1. _____

    _____

    _____

2. _____

    _____

    _____

3. _____

    _____

    _____

4. _____

    _____

    _____

5. _____

    _____

    _____

CREDIBILITY

Worksheet 2 Is Your *Credibility* Based On What Counts?

Activity vs. Impact

As we take a closer look at the factors you listed in Worksheet 1, we need to decide if they are simply an activity, which is easy to measure, or if they reflect the impact you have on the lives of those you serve, which can be far more difficult to articulate. This distinction is important because nonprofit investors are becoming increasingly interested in the external results of an organization and less impressed with internal measures that simply prove the busyness of staff.

➤ Examples of activities (outputs)
- building a new facility
- recruiting and training staff volunteers
- purchasing or upgrading equipment
- number of participants served
- number of classes held
- number of meals, vaccines, bed-nights, etc. provided
- workshop attendance
- acres conserved
- number of children who passed through the facility
- brochures distributed

➤ Examples of impact (*Outcomes*)
- number of children who were born healthy because of proper prenatal care
- number of jobs created because of industrial recruiting efforts
- number of young people who developed an appreciation of the arts and became professional artists because of early exposure and access to museums and galleries
- number of kids not arrested because of proactive afterschool programs
- population increase in ducks because of the number of acres of wetlands that were conserved
- increase in earnings of graduates because what they learned in the program made them more employable
- number of people living longer because of the training that helped them make healthier choices
- number of people able to retain their job—or get promoted—because of the training delivered

A. List the five factors from Worksheet 1 below. Mark if you believe they reflect an **Activity** undertaken by your organization or an actual **Impact** on those you serve.

Credibility Factor	Activity	Impact
1. _____	☐	☐
2. _____	☐	☐
3. _____	☐	☐
4. _____	☐	☐
5. _____	☐	☐

B. Now think about whether these factors are improving/growing and therefore enhancing *Credibility* or deteriorating/shrinking and therefore detracting from *Credibility*...and why.

Credibility Factor	Improving	Deteriorating
1. _____	☐	☐

Why? _____

| 2. _____ | ☐ | ☐ |

Why? _____

| 3. _____ | ☐ | ☐ |

Why? _____

| 4. _____ | ☐ | ☐ |

Why? _____

| 5. _____ | ☐ | ☐ |

Why? _____

CREDIBILITY

Worksheet 3 Where Is Your *Credibility* Focused?

Primary Customers vs. Supporting Customers

Your organization may have tremendous *Credibility* with one group yet very little with another. Determining where your *Credibility* is focused will help determine how much work needs to be done to further develop *Asking Rights*.

➢ **Primary:** The lives directly affected by the work of your organization.
➢ **Supporting:** Those who make the work possible (investors, volunteers, staff, board members, etc.).

List your *Credibility* factors below and then decide on which customer they are focused.

Credibility Factor	Primary	Supporting
1. _____	☐	☐
2. _____	☐	☐
3. _____	☐	☐
4. _____	☐	☐
5. _____	☐	☐

Asking Rights are focused on Supporting Customers. If you find that most of your factors are focused on Primary Customers, then you need to refocus on opportunities to build *Credibility* with your Supporting Customers.

How will changing the focus of your *Credibility* factors allow Supporting Customers to be more fully realized in a fundraising context? Which factors need to be changed? How?

_____

_____

_____

_____

_____

CREDIBILITY

Worksheet 4 Is Your Perspective Accurate?

Internal vs. External Perspective

More than the previous exercises in this section, this worksheet may require time for research as well as discussions with internal and external audiences. The internal perspective is, of course, how the organization views itself and should include discussions with senior staff. The board perspective provides feedback from those close to the organization but not in the trenches of every day delivery of the mission. The last but most critical perspective is the external one...the outsiders. This last group offers an unadulterated, objective, absolute reality check of your organization. You can't argue with them and you can't defend yourself against them. You have to accept their perspective at face value and use the feedback they offer to fuel the articulation of your plans for success.

NOTE: If the workshop session is populated with a mix of perspectives, each attendee should answer for him/herself based on his/her relationship with the organization (internal, board, or external). If one group is underrepresented, which is typically the case with the external perspective, an organization can employ any number of ways to obtain this feedback, such as a confidential/anonymous survey or a feasibility study conducted by a hired consultant. [If your organization is contemplating a funding campaign, a feasibility study is highly recommended to save time, money, and the agony of being wrong about your *Credibility*. People tend to get very honest when talking about how you want to use their money.]

A. Rate the following 15 factors from 1 (lowest) to 5 (highest) in terms of *Credibility*. Rate each factor from all three points of view and total the factor in the far-right column.

	Internal	Board	External	Total
1. People recognize we are good at what we do.	_____	_____	_____	_____
2. The community/population we serve supports us.	_____	_____	_____	_____
3. Our track record of service/delivery is good.	_____	_____	_____	_____
4. Our board is strong.	_____	_____	_____	_____
5. Our staff is highly qualified.	_____	_____	_____	_____
6. Our 'brand' is well-known.	_____	_____	_____	_____
7. We have national affiliations/accreditations that are assets.	_____	_____	_____	_____
8. We receive outside awards/formal recognition.	_____	_____	_____	_____

	Internal	Board	External	Total
9. The personal reputation of our visible leadership is good.	_____	_____	_____	_____
10. We are viewed as a growing organization.	_____	_____	_____	_____
11. Our fundraising goals are met or exceeded.	_____	_____	_____	_____
12. Our fundraising is viewed as successful.	_____	_____	_____	_____
13. People understand the important role we play in the community.	_____	_____	_____	_____
14. We are fiscally responsible.	_____	_____	_____	_____
15. People want to help us/see us succeed.	_____	_____	_____	_____
Total (for each perspective)	_____	_____	_____	

B. Are internal scores higher than board scores? Are external scores the lowest of the three? If the scores are close together or far apart...why?

_____

_____

_____

_____

_____

_____

CREDIBILITY

Worksheet 5 Should You Improve Weaknesses Or Double Down On Strengths?

You now have some choices to make. Would it be more valuable in terms of funding for you to improve your weaknesses or enhance those things you view as strengths? Which would have a more direct impact on Supporting Customers? Would it be more effective to improve on something you're not very good at or make what you do well even better?

A. List the top three factors from Worksheet 4 that have the highest scores.

1. _____

2. _____

3. _____

B. List the top three factors from Worksheet 4 that have the lowest scores.

1. _____

2. _____

3. _____

C. List the top three factors from Worksheet 4 that have the largest gaps (between any perspective).

1. _____

2. _____

3. _____

Remember...this is about building *Credibility* to achieve *Asking Rights.* Based on what you've listed for A, B, and C, what are the best factors to help accomplish that? Do they focus on improving strengths or shoring up weaknesses? Can you tackle some—or all—of both?

Additional Considerations
- Is the factor a short-term issue, long-term issue...or both?
- Can it be done under the current budget or does it require additional resources?
- Who is responsible for implementation? Is the factor already part of someone's job description?
- How will you measure success?

D. List three factors on which you will focus to build *Credibility* for your Supporting Customers.

1. _____

2. _____

3. _____

CREDIBILITY

INGREDIENT CHECKUP

Before you move into the next section, make sure you can answer each question below with a resounding "yes." If you can't, it would serve your organization well to revisit the areas that need attention before moving forward.

	Yes	No
1. Have you identified what gives you *Credibility?*	☐	☐
2. Is your *Credibility* based on Impact versus Activity?	☐	☐
3. Is your *Credibility* focused on Supporting Customers?	☐	☐
4. Is your perspective on *Credibility* realistic?	☐	☐
5. Have you identified the best course(s) of action to improve *Credibility?*	☐	☐

F = FUNDRAISING SKILLS

Definition (*skills*)	The ability to use one's knowledge effectively and readily in execution or performance [ii]
Critical Fundraising Advantage	It closes the deal
Time Reference	Present
Encompasses	Campaign structure, process management, cultivation, leadership recruitment, correct evaluations, ability to leverage investments, the ask

This second critical component is what allows the other two components—*Credibility* and *Outcomes*—to be monetized. This component is most important when significant, in-person asks will be in your future. More than any other ingredient, *Fundraising Skills* seems to be the area where it is too easy to become distracted. Instead of focusing on the right people and the right strategy to create the right environment for successful asks, too often an organization allows its attention to be diverted by pointless details, superfluous demands, special events, or the belief that expensive software is necessary to be effective.

The general themes these skills center around include management of the process, getting the right people behind the effort, and making the ask. Specifically, the types of *Fundraising Skills* I am referring to are explained below.

➤ Overall Campaign Management

This is the skill of herding all of the cats involved in a campaign. Campaigns, even when managed by outside professionals, still belong to the organization. It is their campaign, not that of the outside counsel or consultants. The 'cats' are those leaders who are the names and faces of the effort, most of whom have day jobs and limited time to devote to the nonprofit. Remember, these leaders are volunteers who represent Supporting Customers and, more important, they are your investors.

➤ Leadership Cultivation

Leadership is critical to the success of the campaign, but even the best leaders will not earn the organization *Asking Rights* if the other components are missing. Much of the early stages in a campaign is spent getting the right people involved because, without them, campaigns can be difficult (if not doomed from the start).

➤ Leadership Enlistment

This is 'signing them up' in two distinct respects: their commitment to the effort and their financial commitment. In most cases, they cannot be leaders of the campaign unless they are also investors.

➤ Correct Evaluation of Prospects

This is the skill that ensures no money is left on the table. After all, it is easy to get $1,000 from someone who really has the potential for a $500,000 investment. Since everyone calibrates to the leaders, it is vitally important that the leaders are asked for the correct amounts or the campaign could be doomed failure.

➤ Interpersonal Skills

These are the skills of communication, the ease with which someone presents themselves, the ability to listen, the art of conversation, the ability to build rapport, etc. These skills are always important when asking someone for something. Self-confidence and pride in one's appearance, though basic, also fall into this category.

➤ Ability to Leverage Investments

An investment from one prospect can be used as leverage for others including, but not limited to, the typical matching grant or challenge pledge. For example, if one bank is interested, others may be as well. Understanding how investments can be leveraged within the same industry (e.g., banks), geographic area (e.g., counties), and size of company (e.g., major employers) can often build a solid campaign foundation.

➤ Organizational Skills

Although it may sound easy, the task of scheduling appointments and juggling meetings can be daunting. In a typical campaign, there may be anywhere from 80 to 140 investors, which means probably 200 different prospects. If each one is met with three times, that's 600 meetings over the course of several months. Add to that the fact that each meeting takes prep work, travel time, etc., and you can see the importance of this skill.

➤ Ability to Make the Ask

In order to raise money, you have to ask for it. Simple to say, difficult (for many people) to do. In fact, asking for money likely ranks along with public speaking and death among people's greatest fears.

The skills above are addressed specifically in Worksheet 8. But before we get there, let's examine your current goals and track record.

FUNDRAISING SKILLS

Worksheet 6 Where Are You Financially And Where Do You Want To Be?

Very few members of a nonprofit's staff or board will say the organization does not need more funding, and the ideas for how to approach this challenge may vary greatly based on point of view. The first step, no matter what approach is pursued, is establishing a baseline for the discussion.

A. Source of Funds: Describe your current annual budget by the following sources/channels, then list your desired or ideal mix of sources/channels.

	Current $	Desired $	Current %	Desired %
1. Annual campaign	_____	_____	_____	_____
2. Membership dues	_____	_____	_____	_____
3. Grants	_____	_____	_____	_____
4. Special events	_____	_____	_____	_____
5. Capital campaign	_____	_____	_____	_____
6. Planned giving	_____	_____	_____	_____
7. Fees for service	_____	_____	_____	_____
8. Other (raffles, auctions, etc.)	_____	_____	_____	_____
Totals (%s must equal 100)	_____	_____	_____	_____

B. What—or who—is the primary driver in the discussion for increased funding? Is it increased demand? Budget cuts? Board pressure?

_____

_____

_____

_____

FUNDRAISING SKILLS

Worksheet 7 What Is Your Organization's Track Record?

Success often leaves clues. So does failure. An organization's track record in fundraising often shapes its view of the future, and nonprofit board members often let the memory of failed efforts haunt their thinking as to what might work moving forward.

A. Does your organization consistently hit its fundraising goals? ☐ Yes ☐ No

From your point of view, is this because of (check all that apply)...
☐ budget?
☐ *Fundraising Skills*?
☐ staff?
☐ external environment?
☐ lack of prospects?
☐ timing?
☐ messaging?
☐ positioning?
☐ other: _____?

B. What do you believe are the top three reasons?

1. _____

2. _____

3. _____

C. Would board members answer the question above the same way? Would the public perception be the same? Why or why not?

_____

_____

Fundraising Skills

Worksheet 8 What Is Your Skill Set?

This self-assessment will help evaluate *your* abilities regarding the most important skills necessary to develop *Asking Rights*. For each skill listed below, write a 'P' for those you personally embody and a 'T' for those you do not but are present in someone on the team responsible for raising money. If neither you nor one of your fundraising colleagues embodies a particular skill, leave the line blank.

P or T

Overall Campaign Management

Previous experience with managing a campaign _____

Current workload permits the time commitment needed _____

Ability to multitask _____

Leadership Cultivation

Successfully cultivated prospects to invest in organizations previously _____

Successfully identified, targeted, and approached leadership
   prospects in a funding context _____

Comfortable in a variety of networking and social situations _____

Leadership Enlistment

Successfully recruited volunteer leaders to fill
   specific roles/fulfill specific duties _____

Comfortable in securing financial commitments commensurate
   with leadership roles _____

Can explain roles/duties required of leaders _____

Correct Evaluation of Prospects

Have a formal evaluation procedure in place _____

Can properly evaluate prospects for the proper level of investment _____

Can assemble appropriate group of people who have knowledge of
   annual giving practices and amounts _____

Interpersonal Skills

Professional demeanor and appearance _____

Good communication skills _____

Ability to think and speak professionally on the spot _____

Ability to Leverage Investments
    Understand the sequential nature of solicitations, which should go from large
        to small amounts (often referred to as the top-down approach)   _____
    Not afraid of critical conversation   _____
    Can reference other investments without divulging personal
        and/or private, confidential information   _____

Organizational Skills
    Can direct administrative staff to set appointments, conduct mailings, etc.   _____
    Ability to make up to five personal visits per day with necessary preparation   _____
    Can establish necessary benchmarks and timelines over
        a multi-month campaign   _____

Ability to Make the Ask
    Confident in ask amount, knowing that it will be met with surprise
        or disagreement   _____
    Ability to explain why investment is necessary   _____
    Can drill deeper if met with "no" to turn it around to a "yes" next time   _____
    Skilled at leaving door open for next steps and follow up   _____

There is no definitive score for this exercise. It is designed to surface the areas where skills are needed or need improvement. While each skill is important, some are more easily improved than others. For example, some people may be very good at cultivating prospects in social settings, but they get cold feet when it comes to actually asking for money.

Some questions to ask yourself...
- Which of the sections/skills need the most attention for your organization to succeed in its funding efforts?
- Are these areas easily improved or is a major overhaul necessary?
- Can staff be trained...or can the problem areas be solved with outside counsel?

FUNDRAISING SKILLS

Worksheet 9 How Will You Fill In The Gaps?

Based on the areas that surfaced in Worksheet 8, how are you going to shore up your *Fundraising Skills* so that you can successfully raise money? This worksheet is designed to further the discussion so that decisions can be made and proactive steps can be taken.

✓ Step #1: Determine if your organization can/wants to handle the funding effort through internal (staff) or external (consultant) effort. *Note: The dollar signs represent the relative scale of potential costs.*

✓ Step #2: If external, determine if a consultant (part-time or full-time) is needed.

✓ Step #3: Whether internal or external, determine the effort's time and budget needs/constraints.

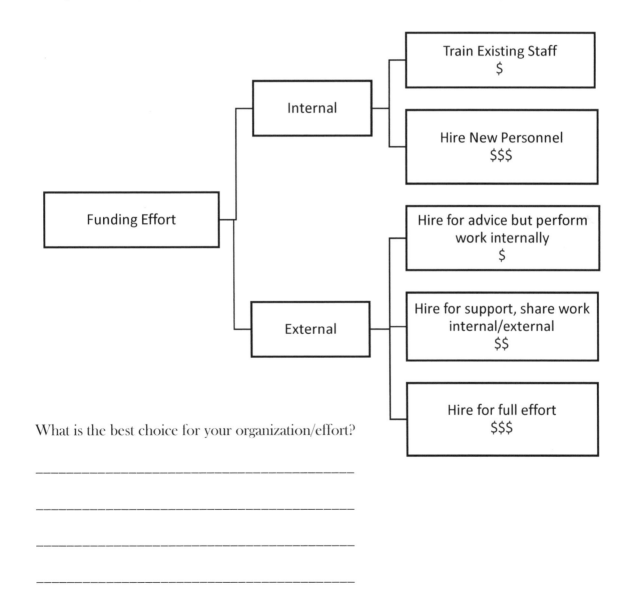

What is the best choice for your organization/effort?

_____

_____

_____

_____

FUNDRAISING SKILLS

Worksheet 10 What Motivations Do You Use?

A big—and often underestimated—part of fundraising is understanding the motivations of your prospects. The messaging you use in your collateral material is a clue to what motivations you are targeting.

A. List the three most common tag lines/messages/themes/campaigns used by your organization in appeals and/or collateral pieces.

    Examples: *Our programs are vital to our continued success.*
                   Improving life, one breath at a time.
                   Change we need.
                   Telling stories that make a difference.

                                                          E or R

    1. _____   _____

    2. _____   _____

    3. _____   _____

B. Now label each with E (primarily an 'emotional' appeal) or R (primarily a 'rational' appeal). As a guideline, if a tag line/message/theme/campaign is vague, an opinion, or uses hyperbole, it is typically emotional.

C. It is fair to say that for decades—and, for the most part, continuing to this day—the de facto appeal used by fundraisers has been the emotional appeal. While this has been effective in the past, the universe of prospects has matured and become more demanding, making it less and less effective. Are you relying too much, even exclusively, on emotional appeals? Have you considered that rational appeals (quantifiable information) can also be highly effective?

What has been your most effective rational appeal to date? Why do you think it is so effective?

_____

_____

_____

_____

_____

_____

_____

_____

FUNDRAISING SKILLS

INGREDIENT CHECKUP

Before you move into the next section, make sure you can answer each question below with a resounding "yes." If you can't, it would serve your organization well to revisit the areas that need attention before moving forward.

1. Have you determined how much money you need to raise?

    ☐ Yes   ☐ No

2. Have you examined your experience in raising money and determined any trends or patterns?

    ☐ Yes   ☐ No

3. Do you or does your team/organization have the skills to manage a funding initiative, recruit leadership, and make the ask?

    ☐ Yes   ☐ No

4. If necessary, will the organization address gaps in your skill set with training, internal staff support, or by hiring outside expertise?

    ☐ Yes   ☐ No

5. Does your organization appeal to both emotional and rational investment motivations?

    ☐ Yes   ☐ No

O = OUTCOMES

Definition	Something that follows as a result or consequence [iii]
Critical Fundraising Advantage	It justifies the amount of the investment
Time Reference	Past, present and/or future
Encompasses	Ability to deliver, effectiveness of operations, implementation, focus, strategy, communication of results

As a review, outputs are typically measures of activity, whereas *Outcomes* are the impact an organization has on its Primary Customer. These are my working definitions and, to be more thorough, we can look to the book "The Nonprofit Outcomes Toolbox" [iv] for further reinforcement.

- *Output*: What your program or organization produces; it is your product.
- *Outcome*: The direct, intended beneficial effect on the stakeholders or interests the organization and its programs exist to serve.

If the program is what we *do* and the output is the *product* of what we do, then *Outcomes* are what happens *because* of that product. *Outcomes* are what raise the ante in the fundraising game. *They justify the amount of the ask.* They are a critical component of *Asking Rights*. If they are based on past accomplishments, they add to the *Credibility* of an organization. To be most effective in a fundraising context, however, they should represent what new investments will make possible.

In Worksheet 2, we learned what are not *Outcomes*. In that same fundraising context, the following <u>are</u> *Outcomes*.
- number of children who were born healthy because of proper prenatal care
- number of jobs created because of industrial recruiting efforts
- number of youth who developed an appreciation for the arts and became professional artists because of early exposure and access to museums and galleries
- number of youth who were not arrested because of proactive afterschool programs
- increase in duck population because of the number of acres of wetlands that were conserved
- increase in earnings of graduates because what they learned in the program made them more employable
- number of people who lived longer because of the training that helped them make healthier choices
- number of people who were able to retain their job—or get promoted—because of the training delivered

OUTCOMES

Worksheet 11 What Are Your *Outcomes*?

In the spirit of The Classic Logic Model embraced by the nonprofit world, list:
- your organization's three largest/biggest (by staff or funding) activities or programs
- the corresponding output of that program/activity
- the *outcome* of that program/activity

Hints
- This exercise is more difficult that it looks. My experience has been that even though this is the most important ingredient of *Asking Rights*, *Outcomes* are often the most difficult to articulate.
- Outputs can be most easily defined as a measure of progress or activity. They are <u>what</u> you do when you are open for business.
- *Outcomes* are defined as the impact that your efforts actually have on your Primary Customers (Worksheet 3). They are often more difficult to measure.

The Classic Logic Model

Program/Activity	Outputs	*Outcomes*
1. _____	_____	_____
	_____	_____
2. _____	_____	_____
	_____	_____
3. _____	_____	_____
	_____	_____

Just to make sure you understand the difference between outputs and *Outcomes:* Do your *Outcomes* represent the end result of your efforts, aka the downstream impacts? Do they describe the impact on your Primary Customer? Be specific. You will refer to these *Outcomes* in future exercises.

OUTCOMES

Worksheet 12 Are Your Efforts Really Devoted To Delivering *Outcomes*?

This is a trick question. The answer must certainly be "yes" because this is implicit in your mission. Below are different ways to look at the question from an outsider's point of view. At a minimum, they can paint a picture that may not be very flattering. At their worst, they can be a major stumbling block to a successful funding effort.

➤ Direct Delivery vs. Overhead

   Is your budget for program/service delivery in line with industry standards? If a funding prospect was given a set of your financial statements or they saw that your organization only received two of four stars from a third-party evaluation, would your overhead look too heavy? Could these factors be perceived as focusing more on building an empire rather than delivering *Outcomes*? Could you easily validate and/or defend that your organization spends the bulk of its dollars on mission-critical activities?

➤ Degrees of Separation

   How many degrees/steps between your outputs and the resulting *Outcomes*? If the downstream impacts are far downstream, does your organization lose the ability to receive credit for the impact actually happening? Can this distance be shortened?

➤ Tracking

   Is it someone's job to actually keep track of your organization's *Outcomes*? It's very difficult to create a value-added, return-on-investment environment if nobody is responsible for this. (HINT: Investors will often pay for this...because it is *that* important.)

➤ Communication

   What percent of your budget is devoted to communicating *Outcomes*? In what ways are your *Outcomes* communicated: newsletter? annual report? website? event(s)? conversations? Is it in someone's job description to not only track the *Outcomes* but to communicate them to investors?

After reading the above...
▪ Taken together, does it appear that your efforts are really devoted to delivering *Outcomes*?
▪ Are these *Outcomes* communicated effectively?
▪ Can you directly connect your funding to *Outcomes* delivered?

OUTCOMES

Worksheet 13 To Whom Are Your *Outcomes* Most Valuable?

While *Outcomes* reflect an organization's efforts to fulfill its mission, their importance in developing *Asking Rights* lies in an organization's ability to monetize them. In other words, how can you make them valuable to your funding targets? Nonprofits, when faced with the need for more funding to deliver their mission, often start their hunt by focusing on who has the deepest pockets. This focus—where the tail often wags the dog in nonprofit funding—is almost always the wrong way to approach sustainable funding. (More on this topic is featured in Worksheet 22). When your *Outcomes* are valued by prospects, funding typically follows. Rather than hope those with deep pockets find your *Outcomes* valuable, it is often more effective to first determine your most valuable *Outcomes* and then match those with individuals, corporations, organizations, and/or foundations that have a natural affinity for them.

Traditional Example
A local arts center needs funding. The center's development staff draws up a list of the usual suspects in the community to approach for funding, with the only common denominator being that these targets—who may or may not have any connection to the organization—purportedly have the ability to write a big check. (In other words, the targets are being approached not because they necessarily value the *Outcomes* delivered by the organization, but because they have deep pockets.)

Better Example
A local arts center needs funding. The center's mission is to provide exposure to art in an area where it would not otherwise exist without them. Students attend classes at the center, patrons attend exhibits there, and the community uses it for special events. Because of these activities, one of the organization's many *Outcomes* is that it helps the community be a more attractive place to live and work, which makes the community more valuable to major employers in the area for several reasons, including happier employees, easier recruiting, and better property values.

List your *Outcomes* from Worksheet 11 and then describe the Supporting Customer who might value them.

Program/Activity	*Outcome(s)*	Who will most value it?
1. _____	_____	_____
2. _____	_____	_____
3. _____	_____	_____

OUTCOMES

Worksheet 14 Are Your *Outcomes* Investable?

What are Investable *Outcomes?* They are *Outcomes* that meet the following five criteria:

1. They pass the 'reasonableness' test.
2. They have a likely chance of succeeding.
3. They provide an acceptable return on the required investment.
4. They allow the dots to be easily connected.
5. They are valued by investors.

A bit more on each...

1. **Do they pass the 'reasonableness' test?**

   Are the desired *Outcomes* or the plan to achieve them reasonable given the type of organization—its mission, size, experience, budget, etc.—in relationship to the amount of investment being sought? Is the price tag of the project/program of work reasonable compared to the perceived value of the *Outcomes* to be delivered, or will the cost cause 'sticker shock?'

2. **Do they have a likely chance of succeeding?**

   Is the organization capable of not just succeeding at the funding effort but at the effort to be funded? Does it have the internal expertise? Is it stretching itself in an area where it has succeeded before or is it falling subject to mission creep? (This is a danger when an organization enters into new markets, programs, or services.)

3. **Do they provide an acceptable return on the required investment?**

   Is the good that will be done by the investment commensurate with the amount of money being sought? Even though it might take some work, can the return on dollars be calculated in terms that matter to the investor? How long will the return take to materialize? Is there more upside than downside, or is the risk limited in any way?

4. **Do they allow the dots to be easily connected?**

   Investors need to be shown, in plain language, how their investment will enable the project/initiative to succeed. In the vocabulary of the industry, do the inputs logically lead to the outputs that then lead to the *Outcomes?* For example, can investors easily see that if a new program is introduced to the local arts center it will lead to the organization becoming financially sustainable (aka the *outcome*) as it has claimed in the ask/materials?

5. **Are they valued by investors?**

   This one is easy: Do your targeted investors even care about these *Outcomes*? For example, if it is an organization that is viewed as one that provides local services, investors will not care that a new office will be opened 100 miles away. Is it something that investors—since they are often faced with many opportunities to share their wealth—will deem esoteric, not necessary, a stretch for the organization's mission, or even frivolous?

For each of your *Outcomes* (Worksheet 13), assess whether they meet the criteria.

1. Does it pass the 'reasonableness' test?   Yes   No

   Outcome 1 _____   ☐   ☐

   Outcome 2 _____   ☐   ☐

   Outcome 3 _____   ☐   ☐

2. Does it have a likely chance of succeeding?

   Outcome 1 _____   ☐   ☐

   Outcome 2 _____   ☐   ☐

   Outcome 3 _____   ☐   ☐

3. Does it provide an acceptable return on the required investment?

   Outcome 1 _____   ☐   ☐

   Outcome 2 _____   ☐   ☐

   Outcome 3 _____   ☐   ☐

4. Does it allow the dots to be easily connected?   Yes   No

    Outcome 1 _____   ☐   ☐

    Outcome 2 _____   ☐   ☐

    Outcome 3 _____   ☐   ☐

5. Is it valued by investors?

    Outcome 1 _____   ☐   ☐

    Outcome 2 _____   ☐   ☐

    Outcome 3 _____   ☐   ☐

OUTCOMES

<u>Worksheet 15</u> How Do You Make Your *Outcomes* More Investable?

The appeal of your *Outcomes* can always be improved and, in some cases, can even be made to seem irresistible. The following is an example of an economic development organization that is conducting a $3 million initiative (campaign) to fund marketing and recruitment efforts in the hopes of attracting new companies to the community, which in turn will create jobs. The prospect in this case is a regional bank.

1. Does this initiative pass the 'reasonableness' test? Yes, it is reasonable to assume that if the initiative works and more companies move into the community, more jobs will be created, the economy will grow, and the bank will benefit from that growth through new customers.

   How can you make your organization's Outcomes so obvious, understandable and compelling...but still be realistic?

   _____

   _____

2. Does it have a likely chance of succeeding? Yes, because the nonprofit behind the effort has successfully recruited companies to the area before.

   Describe how your organization's initiative/program will deliver what you are promising. How can you mitigate the risk of falling short of expectations?

   _____

   _____

3. **Does it provide an acceptable return on the required investment?** The amount being sought should result in three new companies locating to the area within five years. Those companies will employ 800 people earning an average of $35,000 per year. Based on the prospect's (bank's) market share, a normal margin earned on deposit dollars, and a stable economy, the requested investment of $200,000 would seem acceptable.

   How will your organization demonstrate its return on investment? Are there aspects that can be quantified? Is a more general value proposition more appropriate?

   _____

   _____

4. **Does it allow the dots to be easily connected?** Marketing the area leads to businesses being interested in relocating there, pending a good incentive package, of course. These relocations will create jobs that will create demand for mortgages, car loans, checking accounts, etc.

   Is it easy for others to understand how your organization will have a direct impact on the results expected? Can you expand on how the organization impacts the community and point to the value that may not be easily understood?

   _____

   _____

5. **Is it valued by investors?** Every town has a bank in it or nearby. Most, if not all, have a manager whose goal is to grow his/her respective branch, which happens when the economy grows. This initiative helps that happen.

   How will your organization's initiative/program help investors in their respective businesses or the community at large?

   _____

   _____

OUTCOMES

INGREDIENT CHECKUP

Before you move into the next section, make sure you can answer each question below with a resounding "yes." If you can't, it would serve your organization well to revisit the areas that need attention before moving forward.

1. Have you identified your organization's most valuable *Outcomes?*

   Yes ☐   No ☐

2. Can you show that your organization spends most of its funding on delivering *Outcomes?*

   Yes ☐   No ☐

3. Can you describe who will most value your *Outcomes?*

   Yes ☐   No ☐

4. Are your *Outcomes* investable?

   Yes ☐   No ☐

5. Can you make your *Outcomes* more investable?

   Yes ☐   No ☐

PART 2
THE RECIPE

1. Discovering Investor Motivations

2. Translating Your Outcomes To Value

3. Matching Your Value To Investor Motivations

4. Using Campaign Dynamics To Maximize Funding

THE RECIPE

The *Asking Rights* formula describes the ingredients necessary for an organization to earn the right and ability to successfully ask for money. It does not, however, guarantee that a funding campaign will be successful. If *Credibility, Fundraising Skills,* and *Outcomes* (C+F+O) are the necessary ingredients, the Investment-Driven Model is the recipe—the process—that forms a more successful funding effort.

The Investment-Driven Model™

Does the world need another business model? Of course not. But neither do we need another diet book or reality show. Thankfully, the Investment-Driven Model (IDM) is not a business model; it is a completely new way of looking at how to raise money for nonprofits. It is a sustainable funding model (aka a better way to ensure consistent funding over the long term).

Fundamentally, the IDM is based on the following three patterns I have observed during the successful execution of hundreds of campaigns:

- eliminating the gift mentality
- emphasizing results
- relying less on the emotional appeal

These patterns were termed 'paradigm shifts' in my book "ROI for Nonprofits: The New Key to Sustainability" and their characterization still hold today. But there is more to it than shifting a paradigm. It really is a process.

The IDM's foundation lies in concepts introduced in "*Asking Rights*: Why Some Nonprofits Get Funded (and some don't)," namely:

- the difference between a donor and an investor (Chapters 1 and 2)
- the need for more than an emotional appeal (Chapters 3 and 4)
- the importance of the right metrics and demonstrating value (Chapters 6 and 7)

It is also an extension of the logic model that had been a staple of nonprofits, especially in grant funding, which goes beyond the program/activity, output and *outcome* format to include adding the value of those *Outcomes*. The IDM gets to the heart of the matter. It is the process to fully monetize the characteristics of *Asking Rights*.

Like the *Asking Rights* formula, the IDM is deceptively simple. At its most basic level, it only has four phases:

1. Discovering Investor Motivation
2. Translating Your *Outcomes* To Value
3. Matching Your Value To Investor Motivations
4. Using Campaign Dynamics To Maximize Funding

DISCOVERING INVESTOR MOTIVATIONS

Before any appeal or ask can be successful, an understanding of what will motivate an investment in your organization is essential. While this is discussed more fully in Worksheet 18, the next three worksheets will help explore this concept and allow better monetization of your *Outcomes*.

Motivation Pyramid

While there are several 'pyramids' used in the fundraising industry, the one that is useful in the context of developing *Asking Rights* is the Motivation Pyramid. It was first introduced to me through Kay Sprinkle Grace's book "Beyond Fundraising: New Strategies for Nonprofit Innovation and Investment," which describes three types of attributes—or motivations—that must be developed for effective fundraising: connection, concern, and capacity.

➤ Connection — Described as the strongest factor in determining a potential investment, connection was originally tied to an emotional feeling for the nonprofit organization. What is often overlooked is that the connection *can be the value delivered by the organization.* Those who like to see their money used wisely can become connected by the efficiency and/or the effectiveness of the organization in delivering valuable *Outcomes.*

  Example: A man invests in a hospital because it is where his life was saved.

➤ Concern — More intellectual than emotional, this motivation is one of identifying with a nonprofit organization or its mission without being emotionally attached.

  Example: A corporation invests in arts and culture organizations so that the community is more appealing, thereby making the attraction of quality employees easier.

➤ Capacity — Not so much a motivation but rather a qualifying characteristic. This is simply the ability to give.

  Example: A wealthy family with little or no connection or concern for the mission of a particular nonprofit directs discretionary funds to it simply because they are asked, or a company that is solicited because it is located in the general vicinity of the nonprofit.

With the IDM, it helps to think of these motivations in graduating levels. The pyramid (see next worksheet) is useful in demonstrating the concept that each level is built on the one before it. As it relates to funding, that means the potential for investments gets larger as the motivations build on one another. In other words, the largest investments are likely to come from those at the top—the connection level—but there will be fewer of them. And while there may be many in number at the capacity level, their investments will be relatively small.

DISCOVERING INVESTOR MOTIVATIONS

Worksheet 16 To Whom Are You Appealing?

Based on the definitions presented, list your 10 largest investors at their appropriate level on the pyramid.

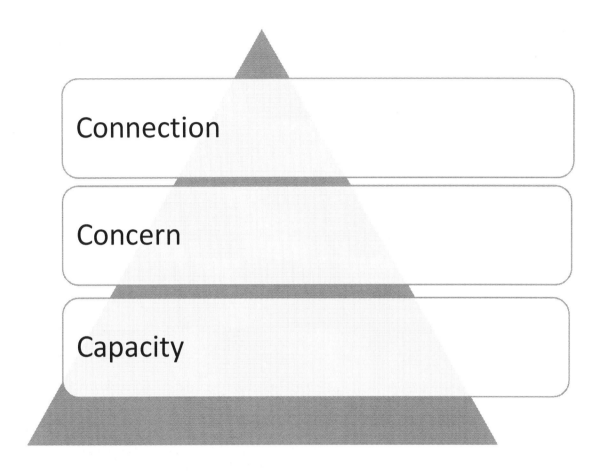

- Are your investors clustered in the top levels? They should be, because they are your largest sources of funding.
- If they aren't, why not? If they're at the Capacity level, there's room for improvement. Connecting them typically leads to more funding.
- Have the more recent investors been more towards the top? Have some that were previously at the Capacity level now become connected? How?

DISCOVERING INVESTOR MOTIVATIONS

Worksheet 17 What Is Your Appeal Spectrum?

The diagram below shows the spectrum of the range of appeals an organization can make to a potential funder and a sampling of how various appeals fit on this spectrum.

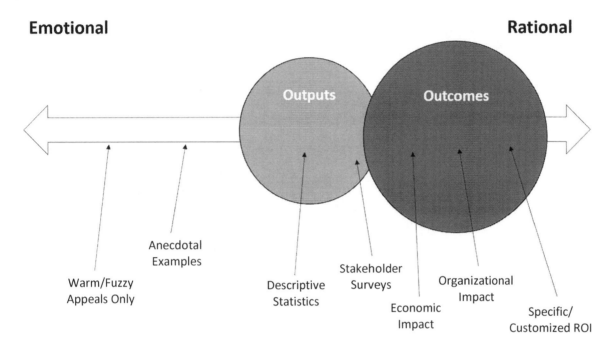

On Worksheet 10, you listed the most common appeals/themes/taglines your organization is using. They may have changed a bit since then or you may have discovered new ones throughout this process. Look at those same appeals...labeled E or R...are they *Outcomes* or outputs? Place your organization's most common appeals where they belong on the spectrum below.

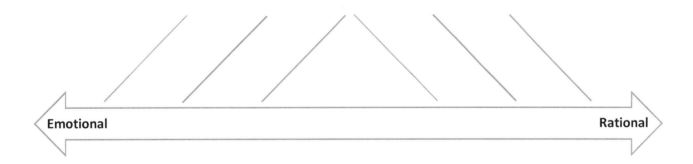

DISCOVERING INVESTOR MOTIVATIONS

Worksheet 18 What Should You Ask Investors?

The only way I know to truly understand the motivations of potential investors is to talk with them. Personally talk with them. Impersonal surveys don't work, and even though your board may be comprised of very intelligent and experienced people, they cannot speak to or know—with certainty—the motivations or financial situations of others.

The ideal vehicle to discern investor motivations is a funding feasibility study. A study doesn't prove that you need to raise money; it proves that you can—or cannot—raise the money you think you need (or sometimes think you deserve). It also fully embodies one of the basic tenants of fundraising:

Before you ask someone for their money, ask for their opinion.

The IDM takes this thought and makes it more relevant to how money is raised in today's nonprofit funding climate by not relying exclusively on emotional appeals. It genuinely asks prospects, or potential investors, for their opinion and directs the discussion to how their opinion can be realized in tangible, non-emotional ways. The goal here is to discover what really interests them and what would motivate them to open their checkbooks—corporate or personal.

Feasibility Study Question Examples
Business/Corporate
- How might your company benefit from our proposed program of work?
- Are there ways our organization could increase that benefit to you?
- How might our organization position its program to make it more appealing to your marketing or business development efforts?
- How important is a tangible ROI to your decision to invest?
- Are there other sources of investment in your organization besides the philanthropic budget where our *Outcomes* may be more valuable to you?

Personal/Family
- Are you more interested in funding for operations, opportunities for facility improvements, or ensuring the organization can weather economic ups and downs through an endowment?
- Are your philanthropic goals more immediate or more structural/long-term?
- Can we have your help in refining our *Outcomes* so that they are more in line with your giving parameters or make more sense to other facets of your family's foundation's goals?
- Do you have any ideas on how this organization can be more effective or thoughts on what would draw you to be interested in financially supporting it?
- Is public recognition important to you?

After reading the above question examples, imagine yourself in a meeting with a potential investor using an emotional appeal to try and extract information and uncover his/her motivations to invest. Tough, isn't it? And the more you try, the more you probably sound like a commercial or advertisement for your organization. Or you may find yourself using one of the better emotionally focused techniques, which is to lead with a negative emotion, offer a solution/relief with a positive emotion, and invite the prospect to help you solve the problem/right the wrong/relieve the pain.

However you formulate an emotional appeal, you will find that you are relying on advertising or sales techniques rather than discovering what is important to the potential investor. The feasibility stage is not for selling your program; it is the time for utilizing those prized listening skills so that you can be open to hearing the critical evaluation of your project/goal/program, which will help lead you to ways that will ensure its funding success.

The funding feasibility study is such an important part of the process that if it's not done correctly, it can severely hamper the campaign, adding to its length, driving up its cost, and, ultimately, raising less money. By uncovering what potential investors are interested in—what motivates them to open their checkbook—you will have something solid on which to build a foundation for funding success.

A. What questions will you ask potential investors that will uncover their views of your *Credibility?*

_____

_____

_____

_____

B. What questions will you ask to determine their views of your *Outcomes?*

_____

_____

_____

_____

C. How will you ascertain their thoughts on the likelihood of investing in your organization without directly asking them for a commitment? (Remember...it is a feasibility study, not a solicitation.)

_____

_____

_____

_____

D. What will you ask to follow up on the above that explores ways to increase the potential of a larger investment?

_____

_____

_____

_____

TRANSLATING YOUR OUTCOMES TO VALUE

Worksheet 19 What Makes Your *Outcomes* Truly Valuable?

The next step in taking the ingredients of *Asking Rights* and combining them into a recipe for funding is to translate your *Outcomes* into value. This is the most difficult part of the process for those who are not 'numbers people,' and it can be daunting. The following worksheets are constructed to help make the concept easier to understand and implement.

A. List your organization's three most important *Outcomes* (Worksheet 11).

   1. _____

   2. _____

   3. _____

B. Use the questions below to clarify the various ways the value of your *Outcomes* might be viewed.

   1. Which *outcome* describes the value of your organization at a broad level?

      _____

      Examples:
      ▪   the impact of your organization (as an entity)
      ▪   community-wide impacts (the word "community" does not carry geographic limitations)
      ▪   constituency impact

   2. Which *outcome* reflects a positive effect that your organization maximizes, enhances, or produces? (This works especially well in education, health, and economy-related arenas.)

      _____

      Examples:
      ▪   children who were born healthy
      ▪   former dropouts who now have a degree or diploma
      ▪   new businesses that employ more people in jobs that pay higher wages

3. Which *outcome* describes a negative cost that your organization minimizes, eliminates, or converts to a positive effect?

_____

Examples:
- people who did not get the disease
- juveniles who did not get arrested
- people who become employable because they now have the skills

4. Which *outcome* reflects a benefit/return on investment to an industry, sector or specific demographic?

_____

Examples:
- less time spent on recruitment and training because the labor pool is deeper
- less costs to law enforcement and the judicial system because more role models are available
- fewer bottlenecks in the healthcare system because of proactive care or systemic insurance coverage

5. Which *outcome* describes the value you add to a program, process, or community?

_____

Examples:
- cost savings because of your particular system or process
- specific talent or expertise unavailable elsewhere
- superior management of situations, which cannot be replicated by others

TRANSLATING YOUR OUTCOMES TO VALUE

Worksheet 20 How Should You Determine Value?

In its simplest form, the value of something today is the value of future benefits. This is theoretically demonstrated by a process called 'net present value.' Technically, it is the following formula:

$$NPV = \sum_{t=0}^{n} \frac{CF_t}{(1+k)^t}$$

Practically, it represents this:

Value today = Value in year 1 + Value in year 2 + Value in year 3 + (ad infinitum)

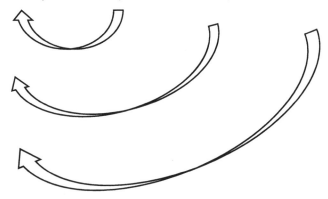

If your organization has the ability to take the calculus of value to this level, it is worth doing...especially if you are talking to bankers, accountants, financial planners, etc. Practically speaking, this is difficult and may not be necessary. Next are two examples that do a fine job of demonstrating value without going to this level.

Applying a formulaic process to value what nonprofits do used to be considered pushing the envelope. Now, nine years after "ROI for Nonprofits: The New Key to Sustainability" was published, it is considered a prerequisite for funding at anything beyond the nominal level.

Example #1 – Positive Effect Enhanced

A program in South Carolina was focused on creating a pool of dollars to be used for local school scholarships so that young people would stay in the area, thereby deepening the workforce. The program also created additional benefits, such as attracting families to the area because of the existence of this innovative program.

➤ New Households: Once the program is fully implemented, an estimated 78 new families per year will move into the area to take advantage of the program. Using a median income of $44,587, this equates to more than $3.47 million dollars per year in household earnings injected into the local economy.

➤ College Graduates: When fully implemented, the program will add an additional 23 Associates and 45 Bachelors degree recipients per year to the area. Using an annual earnings increase over high school graduates of $8,000 per year for an associate degree and $22,000 per year for a bachelor's degree, the following estimates of increased earnings accruing to the area in just one year because of these additional graduates, assuming they reside and work in the area, can be determined.

	Bachelor's	Associate
Number going on to college	45	23
Earning difference vs. high school graduate	$22,000	$8,000
	$990,000	$184,000
Length of working career (years)	45	45
	$44,550,000	$8,280,000

Impact of additional college graduates in lifetime earnings: $52,830,000 (not adjusted for inflation)

Example #2 – Negative Cost Minimized

A national program for teenagers offered many positive impacts, including a lower average pregnancy rate for its participants, which correlated to a host of negative societal *Outcomes* avoided because of the efforts of the organization.

Applying the 2010 four-county teenage (defined as ages 10-19) birthrate of 1.19 percent to the organization's teenage female population of 4,531, it was expected that 54 of these girls would become pregnant. The actual number of program participants ages 10-19 who became pregnant was zero.

What is the value of this extraordinary result?

This broad area of impact is broken down into three more specific areas:
1. Opportunity Value of Staying in School
2. Societal Costs of Teen Pregnancies Avoided
3. Annual Earnings Lost

1. Opportunity Value of Staying in School

According to the most recent information (2010) from The National Campaign to Prevent Teen Pregnancy, only 51 percent of females who get pregnant during their high school years earn their degree compared to 89 percent of females who do not get pregnant. Fewer than one in four teens who has a child before she turns 18 years old has a high school diploma.

What is the value of keeping those teens in school instead of them dropping out because of pregnancy? Using the difference of 38 percent (89 percent who graduate not having gotten pregnant minus 51 percent who graduate after giving birth) and applying it to the 54 girls expected to become pregnant (if service area averages are accurate), the organization impacted 20.4 girls and the associated opportunity costs.

Using 2006 data from The Future of Children, the median annual earnings of females who drop out is $13,255 compared to the $20,650 annual earnings of their graduating counterparts, which equates to 36 percent less. The additional $7,395 earned in just one year by graduates equates to $295,800 per person (unadjusted for inflation) over a 40-year work-life. Applying this to the 20.4 additional teens who do graduate, the total comes to $6,042,166 in added opportunity value. Another positive effect is the teens who do not get pregnant are half as likely to be unemployed and their earnings are much more likely to keep pace with inflation.

Taking this a step further, if they go to and graduate from college, these females will likely:
- earn +$1 million more in lifetime income than a person who does not graduate high school;
- increase their financial rate of return over a high school degree by 10.8%; and/or
- earn 155% more in annual earnings than if they hadn't gone to college.

2. Societal Costs of Teen Pregnancies Avoided

The hard dollar costs of teenage pregnancy are high, including:

- increased reliance on public assistance
- increased health care costs
- increased costs of foster care
- increased criminal justice system costs

Several studies have reported similar findings, including discoveries that show each family that begins with a birth to a teenager is expected to cost the public an average of about $17,000 per year in various types of support over the next 20 years. In present value terms that cost is equal to more than $331,000 per family. Using this figure, if the organization can help prevent 10 teenage pregnancies a year for the next five years, it will provide a present value savings of more than $13.2 million in societal costs.

In terms of tax revenues not generated, it is estimated that teen mothers who do not graduate from high school—therefore earning less over their lifetime—pay approximately 42 percent of the amount that graduates pay per year in taxes.

3. Annual Earnings Lost

While the opportunity costs of not graduating are high, the earnings lost because of not having a degree are substantial. Using the average earnings differential of $7,395 presented earlier for graduating females compared to non-graduating females, the impact of these 20.4 graduates in the local economy is estimated to be $151,054 per year. That is the amount *not* injected into the local economy because of the absence of a high school diploma or equivalent.

A. Can you determine a monetary value for your organization's *Outcomes*? List the most likely *Outcomes* that can be quantified and describe the process that you will use to determine a value that will resonate with potential investors.

_____

_____

_____

B. Are the sources you cite to underpin the validity of your *Outcomes* credible? List the likely sources below. (In the age of instant, unlimited information, statistics can be found to support even preposterous claims, so be prudent in your source choice.)

_____

_____

_____

C. Can you present these values in a simple way so that a prospect can easily digest them?

_____

_____

_____

MATCHING YOUR VALUE TO INVESTOR MOTIVATIONS

Worksheet 21 Are Your *Outcomes* Valued By Your Investors?

A. List your organization's top five funders by name and type.

Examples:

- Jones Company—Grant
- Johnson Bank—Capital Campaign Pledge
- Mr. & Mrs. Smith—Annual Operating Fund Contribution

Funder   Type

1. _____   _____

2. _____   _____

3. _____   _____

4. _____   _____

5. _____   _____

B. For each funder, answer how you know they value your *Outcomes*. Did you ask them? How long ago did you discuss this with them? Have investments gone up? If not, your *Outcomes* are probably being valued less.

Example:

- Funder   *Johnson Bank*
- Last Communication *Informal meeting at local coffee shop*
- Date   *February 26, 2013*
- Discussion Topics   *Used funder's investment to deliver more training (output), had class of 30 and now 22 are employed (outcome)*
- Next Steps   *Invite to annual gala, sit at head table, introduce to mayor*

➢ Funder 1   _____

Last Communication   _____

Date   _____

Discussion Topics   _____

Next Steps   _____

➢ **Funder 2** _____

Last Communication _____

Date _____

Discussion Topics _____

Next Steps _____

➢ **Funder 3** _____

Last Communication _____

Date _____

Discussion Topics _____

Next Steps _____

➢ **Funder 4** _____

Last Communication _____

Date _____

Discussion Topics _____

Next Steps _____

➢ **Funder 5** _____

Last Communication _____

Date _____

Discussion Topics _____

Next Steps _____

MATCHING YOUR VALUE TO INVESTOR MOTIVATIONS

Worksheet 22 Do Your *Outcomes* Drive Funding?

Are funders matched to the *Outcomes* you deliver? In other words, do the *Outcomes* you deliver carry an obvious value to funders? If the answer to this question is "yes," congratulations. Many times, though, they do not. If the answer is "no," then funders are likely investing for reasons other than the *Outcomes* you deliver. This is perfectly acceptable, but those reasons are often dubious and may disappear unexpectedly or without reason.

Example #1 – Two Degrees of Separation from Funding Source to *Outcomes*

The mission of the Smith Family Foundation is to provide educational grants to economically disadvantaged children. The nonprofit organization's program provides educational classes and specialized training to these disadvantaged groups.

➢ Investable *Outcome*: Fifty children a year can attend college who otherwise could not afford it.

➢ Third-Party Funder/Connection: A major employer in the area provides substantial funding to the Foundation because it often hires the organization's graduates. The Foundation, in turn, funds the nonprofit organization so it can continue to provide educational classes that support at-risk youth in their quest to attend college and gain employment upon graduation.

Example #2 – Multiple Degrees of Separation from Funding Source to *Outcomes*

A local nonprofit organization provides education and mentoring on the topic of sustainable agriculture.

➢ Investable *Outcome*: The organization helps create five small farms per year that deliver fresh, healthy, and sustainable produce to local consumers and restaurants.

➢ Funder/Connection: Each local farmer creates 15 new jobs in their respective community.

➢ Funder/Connection: These 15 new jobs not only improve the area's economy, they also improve the quality of life in the area because restaurants serve healthier food.

➢ Funder/Connection: The local businesses financially support this nonprofit because its mission directly impacts the creation of new business/jobs; improves quality of life; diversifies the area's economy; and brings businesses and consumers together through healthy living products.

A. Connect the dots for how your *Outcomes* are related to your funders.

From Worksheet 4, list *Outcome* #1: _____

From Worksheet 6, list the funder that is most closely connected to this *outcome*...and why.

_____

_____

_____

B. Now knowing more about your organization's *Outcomes*, who else might value this outcome and be a potential funder?

_____

_____

C. Can the distance between the *Outcome* and potential future funder be shortened? How?

_____

_____

_____

_____

USING CAMPAIGN DYNAMICS TO MAXIMIZE FUNDING

Worksheet 23 Where Do You Have Investor Leverage?

The leverage I am talking about is the ability to influence others to financially rally behind your cause. Having an idea of who might lead the funding effort as well as those who can be influenced by them will help determine the cost, length of time, and, ultimately, the success of a campaign. The purpose of this exercise is to populate a campaign leadership team, even though much work will need to be done to make it a reality.

The example below illustrates how this might be envisioned.

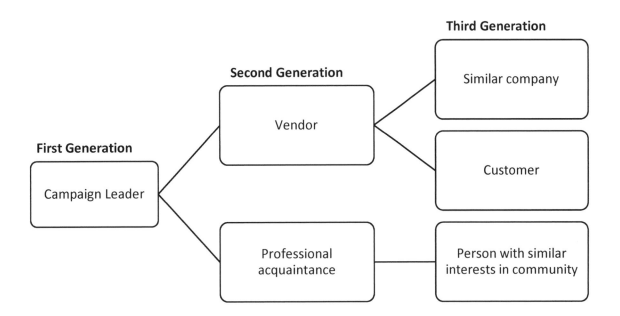

Being a Campaign Leader is a big undertaking. If and when you approach potential leaders with the opportunity to ask their friends for money, many will not agree to the task. For the purposes of this exercise, assume that they will not *directly* be involved in an ask to their friends.

A. List the five most likely people to lead your organization's capital campaign effort. They should correlate to the top five financial commitments.

First Generation

1. _____

2. _____

3. _____

4. _____

5. _____

B. For each of these First Generation candidates, who are those who might be influenced by them? For example, vendors, suppliers, customers, peers, personal friends, competition, etc.? Do this same exercise for the second and third generation of potential investors.

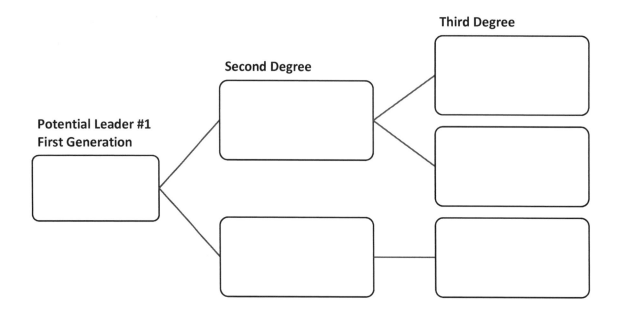

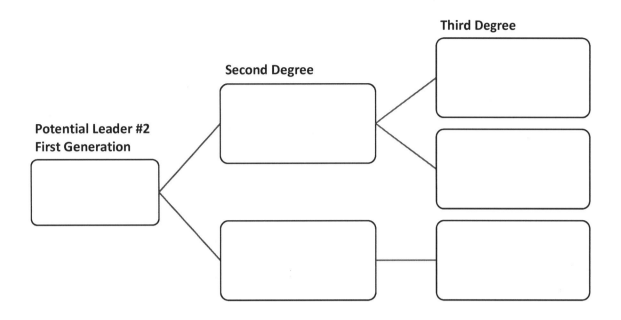

**Potential Leader #2
First Generation**

Second Degree

Third Degree

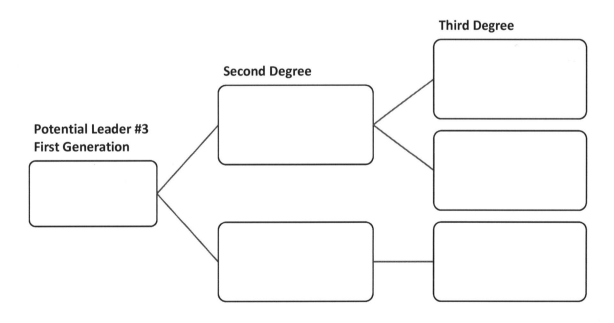

**Potential Leader #3
First Generation**

Second Degree

Third Degree

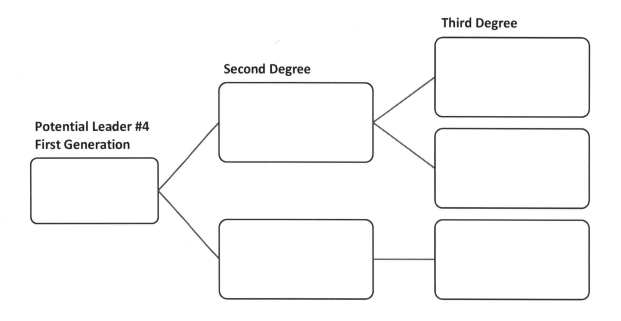

Third Degree

Second Degree

Potential Leader #4
First Generation

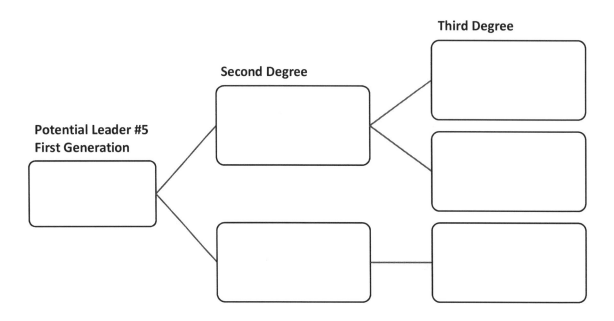

Third Degree

Second Degree

Potential Leader #5
First Generation

If this exercise is difficult to complete...if you can't think of five candidates for top leadership and financial potential...then that points to the fact that a successful campaign might not be in your organization's immediate future. It may reflect on the *Credibility* of the organization or it may be an indicator of the need for board development. Or it may simply mean that the organization has not been paying enough attention to the Supporting Customers who ultimately hold the keys to helping mission-critical initiatives.

C. Were you able to get to the third generation for each of the top five leaders you listed? This would equate to at least 15 additional people who could serve as leaders for your funding initiative. If not, what steps will you take to begin the cultivation of potential leaders?

USING CAMPAIGN DYNAMICS TO MAXIMIZE FUNDING

Worksheet 24 How Will Investors Calibrate To Each Other?

One of the often-underutilized aspects of campaign dynamics is the ability to use the interaction between investors—the dynamic they create among themselves—to raise each other's sights for larger investments. For example, when a smallish banker in the area commits a relatively large investment to an initiative, it is human nature, especially among competitive business people, to feel that a bank five times the size of the smallish one should make an investment five times as large.

The process of identifying the investment potential of a large pool of prospects is called 'evaluation.' An Evaluation Committee is assembled to help formulate these initial impressions of prospects (those with connection, concern, and capacity) and suspects (those with capacity but typically no concern or connection) for investment. The Committee should be comprised of those who are familiar with the organization, the giving climate of the organization's industry or community, and/or have specific knowledge of previous giving patterns of likely suspects and prospects in the organization's service area.

No matter the dollar figure of any given initiative, investment patterns emerge that repeat campaign after campaign in communities large, small, and every size in between. An example of the types of investments needed for a $15 million effort is shown below.

Required Levels of Investment
for
XYZ Initiative

$14.88 million
5 Year Pledge Period

Pledge Amount	Number of Pledges Needed	Amount per Year	Cumulative Totals	
			Pledges	Amount
$3,000,000	1	$ 600,000	1	$ 3,000,000
$1,500,000	1	$ 300,000	2	$ 4,500,000
$1,000,000	1	$ 200,000	3	$ 5,500,000
$ 500,000	5	$ 100,000	8	$ 8,000,000
$ 250,000	10	$ 50,000	18	$ 10,500,000
$ 100,000	18	$ 20,000	36	$ 12,300,000
$ 50,000	25	$ 10,000	61	$ 13,550,000
$ 25,000	54	$ 5,000	115	$ 14,900,000
Totals	**115**			**$ 14,900,000**

After a funding feasibility study, which typically includes 50 to 100 personal interviews, the Evaluation Committee helps expand this potential pool of investors to approximately two or three times the study count and includes the relationships identified in Worksheet 8. The relationships aid in opening doors, establishing initial contact, and sometimes even setting up meetings for formal 'ask' presentations.

Can you envision 300 potential prospects for funding? Why 300? Because you may only get one out of three opportunities to make an ask. A rule of thumb in fundraising that has stood the test of time is that the lead investment needs to be at least 10 percent of the overall goal. You can see in the investment chart presented in this worksheet that the lead amount was almost 20 percent.

Do you have one or more '10 percent' prospects who can lead the way? List them below. If only one, it is critical that you convert this prospect to an investor or the campaign will likely struggle.

1. _____

2. _____

3. _____

4. _____

5. _____

6. _____

7. _____

8. _____

9. _____

10. _____

USING CAMPAIGN DYNAMICS TO MAXIMIZE FUNDING

Worksheet 25 How Will You Make Campaign Leaders Own The Campaign?

Crucial to the success of any funding campaign is ownership of the effort by its leadership. This is even more critical when the organization is relying on a volunteer-driven model of fundraising, which often puts a stack of pledge cards into the board's hands and expects those individuals to do the heavy lifting through in-the-trenches, face-to-face solicitations.

This last worksheet offers questions to test your organization's reality related to the concepts discussed in Part 2. Without the proper foundation laid, leaders of your organization and/or the community are unlikely to engage their time, talent, and/or treasure.

A. Do you have a good pool of prospects who are connected to your organization? (Worksheet 16)

   Yes ☐   No ☐

B. Do you have a wide selection of appeals, ranging from emotional to rational? (Worksheet 17)

   Yes ☐   No ☐

C. Do you have questions developed that will determine the feelings of potential funders about your organization's *Credibility*, its *Outcomes*, and how the value of those might inspire future investment? (Worksheet 18)

   Yes ☐   No ☐

D. Can you explain what makes your *Outcomes* truly valuable? (Worksheet 19)

   Yes ☐   No ☐

E. Are you able to show funders what their investment in your organization means to the community and/or constituency at large? (Worksheet 20)

   Yes ☐   No ☐

F. Are you prepared to show potential investors the value of your *Outcomes*? (Worksheet 20)

   Yes ☐   No ☐

G. Do you know why your existing investors *are* investors? Do you know how/why they value your *Outcomes*? (Worksheet 21)

   Yes ☐   No ☐

H. Are your *Outcomes* matched to those who truly value them? (Worksheet 21)

    Yes ☐   No ☐

I. Can the degrees of separation between your *Outcomes* and funders be made smaller? (Worksheet 22)

    Yes ☐   No ☐

J. Can you recruit a campaign leadership team that has leverage? (Worksheet 23)

    Yes ☐   No ☐

K. Can you expand the pool of potential investors so it is large enough for a successful campaign? (Worksheet 24)

    Yes ☐   No ☐

L. Do you feel you have multiple prospects or one 'can't fail' 10 percent lead investment for your initiative? (Worksheet 24)

    Yes ☐   No ☐

NOTES

NOTES

NOTES

AFTERWORD

According to the National Center for Charitable Statistics, there are more than 1.5 million tax-exempt organizations registered in the United States. That means the competition for 'time, talent, and treasure' is fierce. More than that, volunteers and investors are becoming increasingly savvy—and choosy!—about where they spend their resources.

Asking Rights is not an abstract concept. It is a proven strategy that—when embraced and employed by the various stakeholders of a nonprofit—can bring about remarkable change. Organizations that embrace this methodology become financially sustainable; find new sources of revenue; are able to fund new initiatives; become more accountable and transparent; can more easily test new initiatives for support; are able to recruit new leadership; deliver more meaningful *outcomes*; and become true community assets.

The exercises in this workbook are critical and timely for any nonprofit that wants to not just survive, but thrive. They are designed to keep the perspective of the nonprofit investor in mind, which is critical for long-term success. Adopting the perspective of the nonprofit investor does not guarantee success, but not doing so guarantees a struggle to fully fund your mission and jeopardizes your ability to deliver valuable *outcomes*.

My hope is that this workbook challenges you and your organization to stretch beyond its current thinking to achieve the greater impact that your mission deserves.

About The Author

Tom Ralser pioneered the concept of applying for-profit principles to nonprofit fundraising. Through this methodology he has helped organizations raise more than $1.8 billion over the past two decades by focusing on the outcomes they deliver, which is ultimately why people invest in nonprofits. His Investment-Driven Model™ of fundraising eventually led him to develop the Organizational Value Proposition®, which is now widely used by corporations, foundations, and individuals as a litmus test to ensure the organizations in which they invest are truly delivering outcomes with value.

Having worked with hundreds of nonprofits and in all 50 states, Tom is a frequent keynote speaker and session leader at statewide and national conferences. He is a founding partner of Convergent Nonprofit Solutions, a Chartered Financial Analyst, and author of two best-selling books—2007's "ROI for Nonprofits: The New Key to Sustainability" and 2013's "*Asking Rights*: Why Some Nonprofits Get Funded (and some don't)."

For more information, please visit www.ConvergentNonprofit.com or www.AskingRights.com.

REFERENCES

[i] "Credibility," *Merriam-Webster Dictionary*, Retrieved on March 17, 2013 from http://www.merriam-webster.com/dictionary/f

[ii] "Skill," *Merriam-Webster Dictionary*, Retrieved on March 17, 2013 from http://www.merriam-webster.com/dictionary/skill

[iii] "Outcome," *Merriam-Webster Dictionary*, Retrieved on March 17, 2013 from http://www.merriam-webster.com/diction-ary/skill

[iv] Robert Penna, *The Nonprofit Outcomes Toolbox* (Hoboken: John Wiley & Sons, 2011), 19.

[v] Kay Sprinkel Grace, *Beyond Fund Raising: New Strategies for Innovation and Investment in Nonprofits.* (New York: John P. Wiley & Sons, 1997 & 2005

Made in the USA
Columbia, SC
21 December 2017